The Dalai Lama
Peacemaker from Tibet

Chris Gibb

HODDER
Wayland

an imprint of Hodder Children's Books

© 2002 White-Thomson Publishing Ltd

Produced by White-Thomson Publishing Ltd
2/3 St Andrew's Place, Lewes, BN7 1UP

Editor: Anna Lee
Cover Design and Inside Design: Tim Mayer
Picture Research: Shelley Noronha – Glass Onion
Pictures
Proofreader: Philippa Smith
Cover: The Dalai Lama in 1996
Title Page: The Dalai Lama in Mussoorie, India, in
1959

First published in Great Britain in 2002 by Hodder
Wayland, an imprint of Hodder Children's Books.

This paperback edition published in 2003.

The right of Chris Gibb to be identified as the
author of this Work has been asserted by him in
accordance with the Copyright, Designs and Patents
Act 1988

Titles in this series:
Muhammad Ali: The Greatest
Neil Armstrong: The First Man on the Moon
Fidel Castro: Leader of Cuba's Revolution
Diana: The People's Princess
Bill Gates: Computer Legend
Martin Luther King Jr: Civil Rights Hero
Nelson Mandela: Father of Freedom
Mother Teresa: Saint of the Slums
Pope John Paul II: Pope for the People
Queen Elizabeth II: Monarch of Our Times
The Queen Mother: Grandmother of a Nation
Gandhi: The Peaceful Revolutionary
John Lennon: Voice of a Generation
Florence Nightingale: The Lady of the Lamp

British Library Cataloguing in Publication Data
Gibb, Christopher, 1955-
    Dalai Lama. (Famous Lives)
    1. Bstan-dzin-rgya-mtsho, Dalai Lama XIV, 1935-
    2. Dalai Lamas - Biography - Juvenile Literature
    I. Title II. Lee, Anna
    294.3'923'092
Printed and bound in Italy by G. Canale & C.S.p.A.

ISBN 0 7502 4016 4

Hodder Children's Books
A division of Hodder Headline Limited
338 Euston Road, London, NW1 3BH

**The publisher would like to thank the following
for giving permission to use their pictures:**
AKG 18; Camera Press 11, 14, 16, 19t, 19b, 21, 44;
Chris Gibb 20, 22, 31, 32, 34, 35, 37; Corbis (*title
page*) 27, 29, 30, 36, 40; Eye Ubiquitos 7, 13;
Hodder Wayland 17; Hulton Getty 9; Popperfoto
(*cover*) 5, 6, 10, 12, 24, 26, 38, 39, 41, 42; Tibet
Images 8, 23, 43, 45; Topham 4, 15, 18, 25, 28, 33.

Contents

Lhasa Erupts

As evening fell on 9 March 1959, Lhasa, the holy city of Tibet, was gripped by anger and fear. After nine years of occupation by the Chinese, the inhabitants suspected that their beloved spiritual leader, the Dalai Lama, was about to be kidnapped and taken to China as a prisoner.

Before anyone settled down to sleep that night, the people began to arm themselves with any weapons that came to hand. Nobody was going to allow the invaders to steal their Dalai Lama without a struggle.

Communist Chinese soldiers standing guard near the Tibetan border in April 1959.

Before dawn the next morning, thousands of Tibetans streamed out of Lhasa towards the Summer Palace, where the young Dalai Lama was staying. The mood of the crowd was ugly, and despite the Dalai Lama's pleas for them to go home, the people refused. Fighting soon started and before long the surrounding Chinese armies moved in with great force. The Dalai Lama took the bitter decision to escape over the mountains into India. Ten days later, many of the Tibetan people were massacred.

The Dalai Lama has never been able to return to Tibet, but his peaceful campaigning for freedom for his country, and all oppressed people, has inspired the whole world.

'One of the most important things is compassion. You cannot buy it in one of New York's big shops. You cannot produce it by machine. But by inner development – yes!' The Dalai Lama speaking about the importance of respecting and caring for others.

The Dalai Lama (centre, on the white pony) during the long journey to India.

Tibet and Buddhism

Tibet is a vast and beautiful country. Surrounded by mountains, and cut off from the outside world, the way of life of the Tibetan people remained unchanged for hundreds of years.

The Buddhist religion came to Tibet from India in about AD 500. Like the other major religions of the world, its main focus is on compassion. This means being sympathetic to other people's feelings and experiences. Unlike most other major religions, Buddhists also believe in 'reincarnation'. This is the idea that after people die, their spirit returns to earth in another body. They may take the form of another human, an animal, or even an insect.

This map shows Tibet as it was when the Dalai Lama was born.

0   200 miles

0   300 kilometres

CHINA

Kumbum ■

■ Dharamsala

TIBET

◎Delhi

◎Lhasa

NEPAL

INDIA

BHUTAN

BURMA

N

Tibetans soon adopted the Buddhist way of life, and monasteries and nunneries were set up throughout the country. Many had their own 'reincarnated' monk or nun. The first Dalai Lama (the most honoured monk in Tibetan Buddhism) was born in the fourteenth century. He and the following Dalai Lamas were to become the spiritual leaders of their country.

Buddhist prayer flags flutter in front of the beautiful and isolated Yambulagang Monastery.

'For many Tibetans life was hard; but in the life among our mountains there was perhaps more peace than there is in most cities of the world.'
The Dalai Lama writing about life in Tibet before the Chinese invasion.

Early Life

Tenzin Gyatso, the fourteenth Dalai Lama, was born in 1935 near Kumbum monastery in eastern Tibet. His first impression of the world would have been his village – a few stone houses and a simple Buddhist shrine.

His parents were farmers who owned a few small fields of barley. They kept yaks to plough the fields. The yaks also provided meat, leather for clothes and milk to make butter and butter tea. Butter tea was – and still is – a very important part of the Tibetan diet.

'Butter tea, mixed with salt, is the only gift a very poor people can give to a visitor – and give it they do, cup after cup.'
Sir Charles Bell, a British Resident in Lhasa in the 1920s.

Takster, the area in Tibet where Tenzin Gyatso was born.

Each day began in the same way. The children threw back their yak-skin rugs and followed their mother onto the flat roof of the house. There she would light a small fire and make an offering to Buddha. All across the valley came the sweet smell of juniper and the singing of prayers.

Tenzin's family were not rich, but they lived in a community where people looked after each other. Tenzin played like any other Tibetan child – hide-and-seek, flying kites and wrestling with his older brother. Neither he nor his brother had any idea of what lay ahead.

Tenzin's mother would have carried her children on her back, like this Tibetan mother.

9

The Search for the New Dalai Lama

The thirteenth Dalai Lama, (seated, centre) surrounded by his staff in traditional dress.

The Tibetans believe that each new Dalai Lama is the reincarnation of the previous one. The thirteenth Dalai Lama died in 1934, and soon after important religious leaders started looking for signs and visions that might lead them to the reincarnated Dalai Lama.

Members of the search party noticed that the thirteenth Dalai Lama was looking to the north-east when he died. When they visited a sacred lake, they saw a vision of the hills of eastern Tibet. Among the hills was a huge monastery with roofs of green and gold, where a small child was playing outside a house with a light blue roof.

So a party journeyed north-east to the great monastery of Kumbum, and found a house with a light blue roof. Inside was a young child. When he saw the Abbot of Sera, the leader of the party, the child clambered onto his knee. He asked if he might have the beautiful rosary hanging around the elderly Abbot's neck. The rosary had belonged to the thirteenth Dalai Lama. When offered two identical sets of drums, beads and walking sticks, he always chose those belonging to the previous Dalai Lama.

The members of the search party were delighted. His Holiness the Fourteenth Dalai Lama had been found.

'Even as a child ... he radiated calm, which is very nearly unheard of in a four-year-old. He sat through ceremonies which would tax even an adult.'
Ngakpa Chogyam, a Tibetan biographer, writing about the Dalai Lama as a young boy.

Kumbum Monastery, near the Dalai Lama's birthplace.

A Lonely Childhood

The little Dalai Lama was kept safe at Kumbum Monastery for the first year after he was found. Naturally he missed his family and his playmates. The only companion close to his own age was his elder brother. They continued to play and wrestle together in a friendly sort of way. Sometimes they would hide for hours on end, causing widespread panic amongst the monks. The boys had lots of fun watching elderly lamas rush about trying to find them.

The Potala Palace in Lhasa, home of the Dalai Lamas for centuries.

An oil painting of the Dalai Lama as a young child.

12

At last in 1939, just after his fourth birthday, Tenzin Gyatso began the long trip to Lhasa. The journey took many months as there were no proper roads. The new Dalai Lama was enthroned in the great Potala Palace.

Nobody who was at the ceremony could have believed that in less than twenty years the Dalai Lama and many of his people would be forced to flee their country.

Growing Up

As a boy, the Dalai Lama's favourite toy was his telescope.
Perched on the high roof of the Potala Palace, he would
spend hours watching the bustling life of the people below.
His important religious position made it difficult for him to
mix with his people, but he wanted to be one of them.

Religious studies took up much of his time. He excelled,
and was soon a brilliant debater. But he was also interested
in mechanical things, and here he found a friend –
Heinrich Harrer.

*The young Dalai Lama
conducting one of his
first religious ceremonies
at the Johkang Temple
in Lhasa.*

Heinrich Harrer has remained a strong supporter of the Dalai Lama and Tibet. Here he is meeting a Tibetan in charge of refugee children in Switzerland.

Heinrich was an Austrian explorer who had spent two years crossing the Himalayas into Tibet. He became a friend of the young Dalai Lama, and taught him English and geography. Through his friendship with Heinrich, the Dalai Lama began to learn about life outside Tibet.

Heinrich also gave the Dalai Lama a life-long interest in mechanical things. One summer, while the Dalai Lama was staying at the Summer Palace, they took apart and reassembled a motor car. It was a gift from the British, and had taken six months to cross the Himalayas. The Dalai Lama drove it around the grounds of the palace with great delight.

Tibet and China

For centuries an uneasy but special relationship had existed between Tibet and China. Many Chinese had been converted to Buddhism by Tibetan monks, and looked to them for help in religious matters. In return, Chinese emperors offered to support Tibet if it came under threat from other countries.

This all changed in 1910, when a Chinese warlord invaded Tibet. Revolution swept across China a year later and the Tibetans took the opportunity to throw out all the Chinese and declare themselves independent.

Tibetan troops parade in the uniforms they wore before the Chinese invasion in 1950.

Unhappily, for the next forty years most of the rest of the world remained unaware of what was happening in Tibet. During the Dalai Lama's youth Tibet was closed to visitors, and so remained the 'Forbidden Land' for all but a handful of foreigners.

Tibet had cut itself off from the world, and this was to be its downfall. The two lamas who acted as leaders during the Dalai Lama's youth did nothing to modernize the country. Noble families and some monasteries were very wealthy, while many peasants lived in poverty.

When the Communists under Mao Tse-tung won the civil war in China in 1949, Mao announced his intention of liberating Tibet from what he saw as an unequal society. He wanted to add it to the 'big family of the People's Republic of China'. He also believed that the natural resources – forests, minerals and land – could be of great benefit to China.

Chairman Mao, the leader of China from 1949 until 1976. He was determined to bring Tibet under Chinese rule.

'The evil omens multiplied ... and when one day in blazing summer water began to flow from the roof of the temple, the people were beside themselves with terror.' Heinrich Harrer describing how scared Tibetans were at the idea of Chinese rule.

Invasion

In the autumn of 1950, a young British radio operator called Robert Ford spoke to the governor of one of the eastern provinces of Tibet. 'The Chinese cannot hope to reach Lhasa this year,' said the governor. 'They will not try before the spring'. The Englishman agreed with him.

A week later, on 7 October, the Chinese invaded. The young radioman was to spend four years in a Chinese labour camp.

Chinese troops marching across Tibetan highlands in October 1950.

Armed Chinese soldiers guarding Tibetan fighters who have been forced to give up their guns.

The small Tibetan army had no chance. Within weeks the invaders were approaching the capital, Lhasa. The young Dalai Lama, only fifteen years old, was urged by his advisors to take control. His first action was to contact the United Nations, but as Tibet was not a member, his appeal was not answered.

Urged to escape to India, the Dalai Lama made it as far as the border before deciding to return to Lhasa. Although he knew he was taking a great risk, he preferred to face this disaster with his people.

A Chinese communist leader reads a statement to a crowd of Tibetans, ordering that the Tibetan local government should cease to exist.

'As long as the people of Tibet are compelled by force to become a part of China, the present invasion will be the grossest [worst] instance of the violation of the weak by the strong.' The Dalai Lama's appeal to the United Nations in 1950.

Changes in Tibet

Without support from the United Nations, Tibet as an independent nation ceased to exist. The Dalai Lama had no option but to try to negotiate with the much greater force that was occupying his country. In central Tibet, the Chinese at first promised to respect the Tibetan way of life. But in eastern Tibet, they immediately began demanding money and food. They destroyed monasteries and took away people's land and cattle. Fear of famine haunted the land. Before long, the Chinese promises to respect the Tibetans' way of life were being broken throughout the country.

Nevertheless, the Dalai Lama was determined to work with the Chinese. Like them, he thought that land should be distributed more equally. However, he was very worried by their belief that nobody should have any private possessions, and religion should be abolished.

'When the Chinese first came in 1950, they gave the farmers tools and said they had come to help us. But four years later they had taken everything for themselves.'
A Tibetan farmer describing the behaviour of the Chinese in Tibet.

The Tashilumpo Monastery, south of Lhasa, was one of many destroyed by Communist Chinese troops.

In 1954 the Dalai Lama visited Beijing, the capital of China. There he met Mao Tse-tung and other Communist leaders. Although the meeting was friendly, the two parties disagreed with one another about the future of Tibet. The Chinese wanted to rule Tibet. The Dalai Lama believed that change was necessary, but he wanted the Tibetans to be in control of change. The seriousness of the situation came home to him when he made the long journey back to Lhasa. He became aware that his whole country was like a tinder-box waiting to blow up.

The Dalai Lama (second from right) and Panchen Lama (another important Buddhist monk) are welcomed by the Chinese in Beijing. The talks there were not as successful as the Tibetans had hoped they might be.

Tragedy Unfolding

The Chinese didn't understand the strong independent feeling of the Tibetans, but this isn't altogether surprising. Certainly, many Tibetans lived in poverty and life was often difficult.

Yet despite these hardships, it seems that strong traditions and a common religion united the people of Tibet. There has never been a peasant uprising in Tibet, which contrasts strongly with the many revolts that have taken place in China. The differences between the two countries led to misunderstandings that were to have terrible results for Tibetans and their country.

Although the traditional Tibetan way of life was harsh at times, most Tibetans were content to live simply. This farmer is using his yak to plough his fields.

細菌炸弹

人民防空力人民 人民防空靠人民

A Chinese billboard in Lhasa, showing Tibet as a nuclear testing ground and an area of nuclear waste disposal.

Of course, the Chinese had practical reasons for wishing to take over Tibet. They hoped to find precious minerals and make use of timber from the forests. Tibet also has an important geographical position, opposite India and facing Russia. The Chinese were at war with India twice in the 1960s, and were not on good terms with Russia. Tibet was therefore an ideal location for nuclear missile sites.

The Dalai Lama was well aware of all this. But he felt it was worth trying to achieve a meeting of minds.

> *'... what is most important is the fact that we Tibetans and our Chinese brothers and sisters have always been neighbours and must remain so. The only alternative for the future is to learn to get along and live in harmony with our neighbours.'*
> The Dalai Lama on how the relationship between Tibet and China could be improved.

Uprising and Exile

In 1956 the Dalai Lama visited India, where he received a warm welcome. On his arrival in Delhi he made a speech near the memorial to Mahatma Gandhi. Gandhi was the Indian leader who championed the idea of non-violent protest. The Dalai Lama talked about peace.

On his return to Tibet he heard horrific stories of torture and executions by the Chinese army. Some Tibetans were fighting back and these fighters were moving closer and closer to Lhasa. The Dalai Lama realized that his country would not be at peace for some time.

The Dalai Lama (second from right), having laid a wreath on the shrine of Mahatma Gandhi in India.

'Non-violence is the only moral course – this is clearly in accordance with the teachings of Lord Buddha and as the religious leader of Tibet I was bound to uphold it.'
The Dalai Lama

Trucks transporting Chinese troops and supplies make their way towards Lhasa in 1959.

By March 1959 the fighters had arrived outside the city. Their presence was one reason for the fighting that erupted.

The rising anger of his people left the Dalai Lama in a terrible position. He was totally against violence of any kind, but found it hard to criticize his countrymen and women who were fighting in his name. He pleaded with the Chinese for peace, but with no result. Exile was the only option left.

Escape to India

Leaving Lhasa was not easy. After praying for the last time in the peace of his chapel, the Dalai Lama changed into the simple clothes of a common soldier. With a rifle slung over his shoulder, he and a small party slipped unnoticed out into the darkness.

The first few kilometres were very dangerous, for the group had to pass close to the Chinese camp. They then headed for the wilderness of southern Tibet.

The following days were filled with ceaseless riding through sheer valleys and across high passes – a time of discomfort, cold and great sorrow.

During a pause in the long journey to India the Dalai Lama (centre, seated, in dark robes) sits with his guards.

The Dalai Lama (third from left) arrives in India to a warm welcome in April 1959.

Tibetans and supporters of the Dalai Lama waited anxiously, thinking that the Dalai Lama might have been kidnapped or killed in some remote pass of the Himalayas. When he arrived in India, exhausted but relieved, he was given a rapturous reception by the Indian people and the world's press. But the news from Tibet was grim. Many of the Dalai Lama's supporters in Lhasa had been massacred, his palace bombarded, and the Chinese now held all the power.

'There is no basis whatever in history for the Chinese claim that Tibet was part of China.'
The Dalai Lama

Reign of Terror

Prior to 1950, the lives of the Tibetan people had changed little over the centuries. The traditional culture remained strong, and the country was largely untouched by outside influences.

Following the brutal suppression of the uprising in Lhasa in 1959, the Chinese swiftly set about trying to destroy everything that over the centuries had made Tibet unique.

Tibetan soldiers file out of the Potala Palace to surrender to the Chinese Communists in May 1959.

Some Tibetans managed to flee Tibet after the Chinese invasion. This woman was hoping to find safety in Nepal.

'When we saw our most venerable Lamas, who were our 'Gods' just a few days before, carrying human excrement and sprinkling it over a new made Chinese vegetable garden, many shed tears.'
Dawa Norbu – Author of *Red Star Over Tibet*, a book about the Chinese occupation of Tibet.

The Chinese set up government in Lhasa. All those who were thought to have helped or even sympathized with the recent uprising were in danger. Important citizens were humiliated, imprisoned and often shot. Lamas and monks were dealt with especially harshly. Monasteries were emptied and the buildings destroyed.

Nor did the poorest peasants escape. Thousands were hauled off to work camps for supporting the Dalai Lama, or trying to hide their small stock of barley from Chinese soldiers.

Although the United Nations described the Chinese treatment of the Tibetan people as 'genocide', they still took no action against the Chinese.

The Cultural Revolution

In 1966, a movement called the 'Cultural Revolution' was launched in China. One of the aims was to destroy everything to do with the past. Three-quarters of China's historical monuments were destroyed at this time. Previously honoured leaders were spat on and pelted with mud in the streets. Many people from the towns were forced to work in the country.

In Tibet, the Cultural Revolution led to another wave of destruction against Buddhist shrines and monasteries. Communist soldiers invaded Tibet's holiest shrine – the Johkang Temple in Lhasa – and smashed all the holy statues and images they could find. The great monastery of Ganden, near Lhasa, once the home of over 6,000 monks, was reduced to a pile of rubble. Perhaps most heartbreaking of all, sixty per cent of all Tibet's sacred Buddhist literature was deliberately burned. More people were arrested and imprisoned.

Students and teachers march through Beijing during the Cultural Revolution, in support of Chairman Mao. Their banners read 'Raise High Mao Tse-Tung's Thoughts and Great Red Flag'.

The Chinese call Tibet 'the Western treasure house' – with good reason, for the country is rich in a wide variety of minerals, including uranium, oil, coal, copper and gold. The Communists started mining as fast as they could. Forests in eastern Tibet are still being felled at the rate of one truck-load a minute.

The monastery of Ganden once housed over 6,000 monks. It was totally destroyed by Chinese troops.

'The destruction was wholesale and calculated. Every building of religious or historical importance was destroyed . . . It was an attempt at the extermination of an entire culture.'
Simon Normanton, from *Tibet, The Lost Civilization.*

Hope Fades

The death of Mao Tse-tung in 1976 brought a glimmer of hope to Tibetans. The new Chinese leaders admitted that they had caused problems in the country. Representatives of the Dalai Lama were invited to visit Tibet. They were deeply shocked.

Everywhere they saw abandoned monasteries: of 3,500 monasteries and libraries, fewer than a hundred were left standing. Holy images had been broken and defaced.

Worse still was the Chinese treatment of Tibetan people. Even today the difference between the positions of Tibetans and Chinese in Tibet is marked. In the major towns the Chinese now outnumber Tibetans. They usually have the best housing, electricity, water and sewers. Many Tibetans have none of these basic things.

Today Chinese soldiers are a common sight on the streets of Lhasa.

'Nearly everyone you see is Chinese, and the odd Tibetan in the street reminded me of the Australian Aborigines – reduced to a tourist attraction in their own country.'
An Australian tourist in Lhasa in the 1990s.

The brief moment of hope did not last. The Tibetan people were determined to win the right to rule themselves. They had met travellers from other countries, and heard about places in the world where people could follow their religion freely. The Chinese would not give up any of their power, and riots broke out again.

By 1987, Tibetans were again being beaten, arrested, tortured and shot. Thousands fled their country.

Buddhist monks in the streets of Lhasa in 1987, demonstrating against continued Chinese occupation.

In Exile

While Tibetans were made prisoners in their own country, the Dalai Lama was setting up a safe haven for the Tibetan refugees in India. He made his headquarters at Dharamsala, a beautiful old British settlement that lies at the foot of the first towering rock barrier of the Himalayas. The Dalai Lama's most pressing problem was taking care of the thousands of refugees flooding across the border. Groups of Tibetan refugees still seek safety in India today.

Refugees in Dharamsala have come from all walks of life — high Lamas, nomads, nobles, peasants. Many were forced to abandon their families when they escaped. Some of the children who arrive in Dharamsala are orphans.

A view of terraced fields and the snowy Himalayas from Dharamsala.

Traditional Tibetan celebrations such as this 'Lama Dance' in Dharamsala, India, help keep the Tibetan culture alive.

'The Indian Government still shows the greatest generosity, help and understanding.' The Dalai Lama in 2001.

One of the main concerns of the Dalai Lama and his government in exile, is that education, health care and the celebration of Tibetan culture is continued. The majority of refugees left Tibet with nothing and now face all the difficulties of adapting to a strange culture and a different climate. The Indian Government has been very generous, granting settlements and land to refugees in many parts of India.

Long Years in India

The Dalai Lama has taken a personal interest in establishing the Tibetan community at Dharamsala. Schools have been set up so that, for the first time in Tibetan history, children from all walks of life now receive a full-time education.

Handicraft schemes producing beautiful carpets and other traditional objects have been established, providing work for skilled Tibetan men and women. Hospitals have been built and new monasteries founded.

Children studying at the Tibetans' Children's Village in Dharamsala.

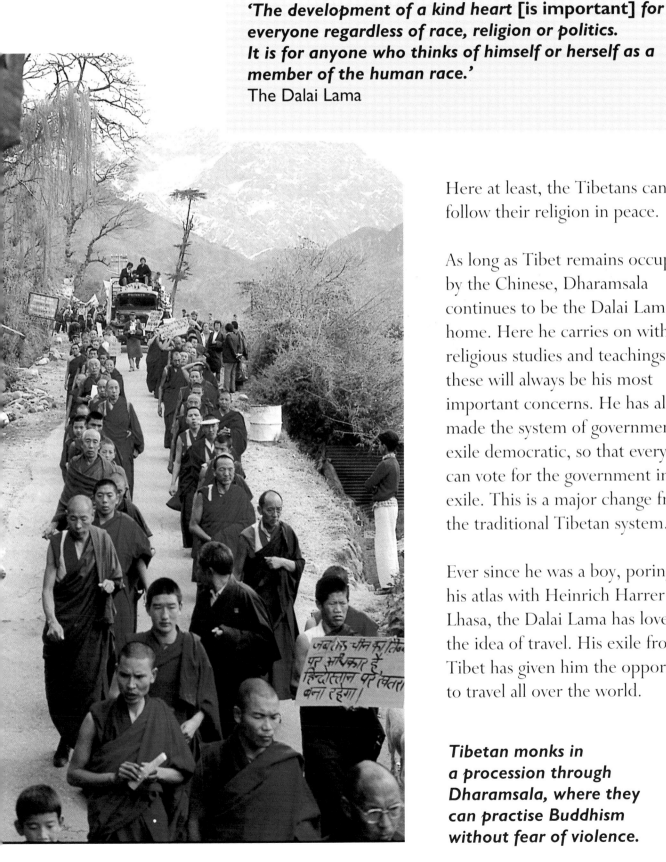

'*The development of a kind heart [is important] for everyone regardless of race, religion or politics. It is for anyone who thinks of himself or herself as a member of the human race.*'
The Dalai Lama

Here at least, the Tibetans can follow their religion in peace.

As long as Tibet remains occupied by the Chinese, Dharamsala continues to be the Dalai Lama's home. Here he carries on with his religious studies and teachings – these will always be his most important concerns. He has also made the system of government in exile democratic, so that everyone can vote for the government in exile. This is a major change from the traditional Tibetan system.

Ever since he was a boy, poring over his atlas with Heinrich Harrer in Lhasa, the Dalai Lama has loved the idea of travel. His exile from Tibet has given him the opportunity to travel all over the world.

Tibetan monks in a procession through Dharamsala, where they can practise Buddhism without fear of violence.

A Universal Appeal

Despite all the suffering of his people and himself, and in some ways because of it, the Dalai Lama has become a truly international figure. He has been invited to many different countries, and people from all walks of life, races and religions flock to hear him speak. Indeed, many of the world's political and religious leaders have spent hours talking with the Dalai Lama.

His message does not concern only the problems of Tibet, although he does feel them very deeply. Nor does he appeal only to Buddhists. Instead, he makes a plea to all people who have a sense of compassion and justice.

The Dalai Lama meeting with United States President Bill Clinton in 2000.

His starting point is that human beings all want happiness and not suffering. This applies as much to nations as ordinary people. Greed and selfishness cause wars; compassion and understanding avoid and heal them.

> *'I believe in tolerance for all – so long as all have a "good heart".'*
> The Dalai Lama

The Dalai Lama praying at the Wailing Wall in Jerusalem, wearing a Jewish yarmulka, or skullcap. The Dalai Lama believes that people of different religions should respect one another.

World Peace

In 1984, the Dalai Lama wrote a book called *A Human Approach to World Peace*. He starts with us – you and me. How do we feel? Do we have a selfish approach to others and use them for our own gain? Or do we try to understand and help our fellow human beings? Only when we can answer 'yes' to the last question can we hope to achieve peace.

> **'If we do not believe that we really are part of one human family, we cannot hope to overcome the dangers to our very existence – let alone bring about peace and happiness.'**
> The Dalai Lama

Photographers from all over the world take pictures of the Dalai Lama as he speaks to a crowd of monks in the Indian Himalayas. People throughout the world are moved by his message of peace.

Inner peace, calmness and compassion are the key words of the Dalai Lama's book. He also asks for a greater understanding between different religions, nations and political systems. Much of the world has an 'us and them' attitude that divides people and countries and leads to war and poverty. The Dalai Lama believes that if we discard such ideas, then we can achieve great things.

The Dalai Lama doesn't have the bitterness one might expect from an exiled leader, who has suffered the destruction of his culture and his people. This is partly what makes his words so powerful.

The Dalai Lama with Archbishop Desmond Tutu, who campaigned against apartheid in South Africa. Although the two men are of different religions, they have similar beliefs about the need for compassion to solve problems.

The Karmapa Lama

In Tibetan Buddhism there are many different religious leaders. One of the most important is the Karmapa Lama.

In the year 2000 the seventeenth Karmapa Lama, aged fifteen, made a spectacular escape to India. His journey was very similar to the Dalai Lama's in 1959. The Dalai Lama was delighted to welcome the young monk to the Tibetan community in Dharamsala.

'He has his own deep spirituality – and cheerful optimism.' Trea Wiltshire writing about the Karmapa Lama in the *Guardian* newspaper in 2001.

Ugyen Trinley Dorje, the 17th Karmapa Lama.

The Karmapa Lama has settled at the monastery of Gyuto, near Dharamsala. He spends most of his day in study and meditation. The monastery has become a place of pilgrimage for many Tibetans.

For many Tibetan exiles the arrival of the Karmapa Lama brought hope. Some think that one day he will take on the mantle of the much-loved Dalai Lama, and help to focus world attention on the plight of Tibetans in exile. The Dalai Lama himself believes that the Karmapa Lama will continue to spread Buddhist ideas and teach people the importance of compassion and peace.

Gyuto Monastery, the home of the Karmapa Lama near Dharamsala.

The Laughing Buddha

'Do you think Buddhism is best?' asked somebody from the audience during a talk by the Dalai Lama in London in 1988. His Holiness laughed, and replied that the Dalai Lama was likely to think Buddhism was best – but it was only best for him, and something else could be best for somebody else. This acceptance of different ideas and religions is something that sets the Dalai Lama apart from many other religious teachers.

Some people make others laugh and smile all the time. The Dalai Lama is one of them. When asked a more difficult question about Buddhism, he cocked his head, wearing an expression that clearly said 'You don't expect me to answer that do you?' He went on to give a talk that left the hall spellbound. He then gave a mischievous grin. 'Well that's what I think anyway.' His sense of humour and constant smile have led some of his followers to call him 'the Laughing Buddha'.

More than 40,000 people gather in Central Park in New York to hear the Dalai Lama speak in August 1999.

The Dalai Lama greets admirers outside a Buddhist Centre in London, England.

'I pay tribute to our brave Chinese brothers and sisters who have also made tremendous sacrifices for freedom and democracy in China.'
The Dalai Lama in 2001, talking about how many Chinese have suffered under Communist rule.

After years of campaigning for Tibetan freedom, the Dalai Lama remains full of courage and hope. For his compassion and concern for all people, and his belief in non-violence in a violent world, he is unique. He was awarded the Nobel Peace Prize in 1989.

Glossary

Abbot The head of a monastery of monks.

Aborigines Native peoples of a country, especially Australia.

Apartheid Racial separation of people – making one more superior to others.

Buddhism The religion that grew from the first Buddha.

Campaign A series of protests and activities designed to bring about change.

Civilization A particularly advanced way of life.

Communism A belief that people should share things equally. Communist countries are often run by a police state.

Democracy A system of government where people are allowed to vote for their rulers, and can express their opinions.

Dictatorship When a ruler holds total power over a country.

Exile A person who has to leave his or her country for ever.

Extermination When something is totally destroyed.

Genocide The deliberate destruction of an entire people.

Independent Free to govern yourself.

Labour camp A prison where people are made to work against their will.

Lama A Tibetan religious leader.

Liberate To free people from invaders.

Monasteries and Nunneries Places where monks and nuns live and pray.

Nuclear missile sites Where weapons of mass destruction are placed.

Persecute To illtreat people because of their beliefs.

Reincarnation Being born into another life after death.

Revolution An uprising against a government.

Tolerance Accepting other peoples' points of view.

Traditional Ways of life that have lasted a long time.

United Nations A world organization based in New York that tries to stop violence and help people.

Further Information

For younger readers:
Buddhism by John Snelling (Hodder Wayland, 1986)
The Dalai Lama by Christopher Gibb (Exley Publications, 1990)

For older readers:
In Exile from the Land of Snows by John Avedon (Wisdom Publications, 1985)
Great Ocean by Roger Hicks and Chogyam Ngakpa (Element Books, 1984)
Seven Years in Tibet by Heinrich Harrer (The Reprint Society, 1953)

Date Chart

AD 500 The Buddhist religion comes to Tibet from India.

1935, 6 July Birth of Tenzin Gyatso – the fourteenth Dalai Lama.

1937 The Dalai Lama is found by a search party from Lhasa.

1940, 22 February The Dalai Lama is enthroned in Lhasa.

1949 The Communists win the civil war in China.

1950, 7 October The Chinese invade Tibet.

1950 The Dalai Lama assumes full power at the age of fifteen. Tibet makes an appeal for help to the United Nations, but is rejected.

1953 Communist reforms are imposed on eastern Tibet.

1954 The Dalai Lama travels to Beijing and meets Communist leaders.

1956 The Dalai Lama visits India.

1956-1959 Revolts continue in eastern Tibet. Tibetan fighters move west towards Lhasa.

1959 The Tibetan Uprising in Lhasa on 10 March. The Dalai Lama escapes to India. The uprising is ruthlessly crushed. Full Communist reforms are imposed in Tibet. The United Nations condemn Chinese atrocities.

1960 The Dalai Lama sets up his government in exile at Dharamsala, north India.

1963 A new democratic constitution for Tibet is issued by the Dalai Lama from Dharamsala.

1966 The beginning of the Cultural Revolution in China. Much destruction in Tibet.

1967 The Dalai Lama makes his first tour to the Far East.

1973 The Dalai Lama's first visit to Britain and Europe.

1976 Mao Tse-tung, leader of Communist China, dies.

1979 The first delegation of Tibetan refugees visits Tibet.

1981 The Dalai Lama makes major tours of the United Kingdom and the United States.

1984 Tibet is opened up to individual tourists. The Dalai Lama writes *A Human Approach to World Peace.*

1984 Ugyen Trinley Dorje, the seventeenth Karmapa Lama is born.

1987 The Dalai Lama suggests a Peace Plan to China. It is refused. Serious riots take place in Lhasa. Tibet is closed again to individual travellers – and has remained so ever since.

1989 The Dalai Lama is awarded the Nobel Peace Prize.

2000 The Karmapa Lama makes a dramatic escape to India.

2001 The Dalai Lama sends a peaceful message to China.

Index

All numbers in **bold** refer to pictures as well as text.